Illustrated Biography for Children

Winston Churchill

Inspiring Tales of a True Hero, Twice Prime Minister

Visit our author page for more children's books
Amazon.com/author/88

Introduction: A Man of Many Hats

Once upon a time, in a land known for its rich history and rainy weather, there lived a man who would become one of the most famous leaders in the world. His name was Winston Churchill.

Now, you might be wondering, what's so special about this man? Well, let me tell you, Winston Churchill was no ordinary person. He was a man of many hats - a soldier, a writer, a painter, and most importantly, a prime minister who led his country through some of its darkest and brightest days.

Winston Churchill was born in a grand palace, but his life was not just about luxury. It was a rollercoaster ride full of adventures, challenges, and incredible achievements. He was known for his fearless spirit, his love for adventure, and his ability to inspire people with his words. Churchill was not just a leader; he was a symbol of courage and determination. He showed the world that with bravery and strong will, even the toughest battles can be won.

A Young Lion

In the grand Blenheim Palace, surrounded by lush gardens and vast parklands, a little boy named Winston Leonard Spencer-Churchill was born on November 30, 1874. He was not just any baby; he was born into a family of dukes and politicians. His father, Lord Randolph Churchill, was a prominent politician, and his mother, Jennie Jerome, was an American heiress known for her beauty and intelligence.

Winston's early life was like a story from a fairy tale, but it wasn't all smooth sailing. He was a curious and energetic child, always ready for adventure. However, when it came to school, Winston found himself in a bit of a pickle. He struggled with subjects like mathematics and Latin, much to the disappointment of his teachers and his father. But Winston had a secret weapon - his love for reading and history. He would spend hours lost in books, traveling to distant lands and times through the pages.

Despite his struggles in school, Winston showed early signs of leadership and determination. He was brave, sometimes a little too brave for his own good. Once, he even had a narrow escape from a near-fatal accident when he jumped off a bridge! But these experiences only made him stronger and more resilient.

Winston's early years were a mix of challenges and joys. He may not have been the star pupil in school, but he had a curious mind and a spirit that couldn't be tamed. These qualities would later shape him into the great leader he was destined to become. Little did anyone know, this young lion was just getting started on his extraordinary journey through history.

The Call to Adventure

As Winston Churchill grew older, his thirst for adventure and his desire to make a mark on the world only grew stronger. After finishing school, he set his sights on a career that promised both excitement and honor – the military. Winston enrolled in the Royal Military Academy Sandhurst, one of the most prestigious military schools in the world. It was here that he trained to become an officer in the British Army, a role that would take him on incredible adventures across the globe.

Winston's time at Sandhurst was a turning point in his life. He worked hard, improved his skills, and graduated with flying colors. Now an officer, he was ready to face the challenges of the battlefield. But Winston wasn't just any ordinary soldier; he had a passion for writing and a keen eye for detail. He decided to combine his military career with his love for writing and became a war correspondent, reporting on conflicts in places like Cuba, India, and Sudan.

One of Winston's most thrilling adventures came during the Boer War in South Africa. He was there not just as a soldier, but also as a journalist, covering the war for a British newspaper. However, his journey took a dramatic turn when he was captured by the enemy forces!

Churchill was taken as a prisoner of war, but his spirit remained unbroken. In a daring escape that sounded like something out of an adventure novel, he managed to slip away from his captors and traveled hundreds of miles to safety, with the help of some friendly locals.

Winston's bravery and daring escape made him a hero back home in Britain. His experiences as a soldier and war correspondent had shaped him into a courageous and resilient man, ready for the even greater challenges that lay ahead. Little did he know, his adventures were just the beginning of a remarkable journey that would lead him to become one of the most iconic leaders in history.

The Path of Politics

After his exciting adventures as a soldier and war correspondent, Winston Churchill was ready for a new challenge. He set his sights on a different battlefield - the world of politics. In 1900, at the age of just 26, Winston was elected as a Member of Parliament (MP) for the Conservative Party. But this was only the beginning of his long and eventful political career.

Winston was not one to stay quiet or blend into the background. He was known for his fiery speeches and his willingness to stand up for what he believed in. This sometimes got him into trouble, and he even changed political parties, moving from the Conservatives to the Liberal Party. But it also helped him make a name for himself as a passionate and determined leader.

One of Winston's most significant roles in government came in 1911 when he was appointed as the First Lord of the Admiralty. This job made him the leader of the British Royal Navy, which was the biggest and strongest navy in the world back then.

Winston threw himself into the job, modernizing the navy and preparing it for the challenges that lay ahead. Little did he know that one of the biggest challenges in history was just around the corner - World War I.

During the war, Winston faced many ups and downs. He played an important role in planning the Gallipoli campaign, which aimed to defeat the Ottoman Empire and open a sea route to Russia. Unfortunately, the campaign was a disaster, and Winston was blamed for its failure. He was demoted and even left government for a while, feeling down but not defeated.

Despite this setback, Winston's political career was far from over. He continued to serve in various government positions, always speaking his mind and fighting for what he believed was right. He warned about the rise of Adolf Hitler and the dangers of appeasing Nazi Germany, even when many others were ignoring the threat.

Winston's journey in politics was a rollercoaster of highs and lows, victories and defeats. But through it all, he remained a fighter, never giving up on his beliefs or his country. His experiences and the lessons he learned during these years would soon be put to the test in an even greater challenge - leading Britain through World War II.

The Darkest Hour

The year was 1940, and the world was in turmoil. World War II had engulfed the globe, and Britain stood on the brink of disaster. At this pivotal moment in history, with the world in turmoil, Winston Churchill became the Prime Minister of the United Kingdom. His leadership quickly emerged as a beacon of hope and resilience, guiding the nation through its darkest hour and cementing his legacy as a legendary leader.

From the moment he took office, Churchill's resolve was clear. He refused to surrender or negotiate with Nazi Germany, despite the overwhelming odds. Instead, he rallied the British people with his stirring speeches, filled with courage and defiance. One of his most famous speeches inspired the nation with a message of determination and resilience, promising to fight in every possible terrain and never surrender.

These words echoed across Britain, inspiring hope and determination in the hearts of millions.
One of the most critical moments of the war was the Battle of Britain. The skies over Britain were filled with the roar of aircraft as the Royal Air Force (RAF) fought bravely against the German Luftwaffe.

Churchill's support and admiration for the RAF were evident when he famously said, "Never in the field of human conflict was so much owed by so many to so few." The courage and resilience of the RAF pilots helped turn the tide of the war, preventing a German invasion of Britain.

Churchill's leadership extended beyond Britain's shores. He understood the importance of forming strong alliances to defeat the Axis powers. He worked tirelessly to strengthen ties with the United States, forging a close partnership with President Franklin D. Roosevelt. This alliance was crucial in securing the support and resources needed to continue the fight against Nazi Germany.

Churchill played a big role in creating the Grand Alliance, bringing together the United States, the Soviet Union, and Britain to fight against Hitler's forces. His ability to work well with these powerful countries showed his great skills in diplomacy and his strong determination to win.

Throughout the war, Churchill's unwavering spirit and leadership were a beacon of hope for a beleaguered nation. His speeches continued to inspire, and his strategic decisions helped guide Britain through its darkest hour to the eventual defeat of Nazi Germany.

Churchill's legacy as a wartime leader remains a symbol of courage, resilience, and the power of the human spirit to overcome even the greatest of challenges.

The Post-War Years

As the smoke of World War II cleared, Winston Churchill found himself facing new challenges in a rapidly changing world. Despite his heroic leadership during the war, Churchill and his party were defeated in the 1945 general election. But Churchill was not one to stay down for long. He continued to be an influential figure in British politics and on the world stage.

In 1951, Churchill once again became Prime Minister of the United Kingdom. During his second term, he focused on rebuilding Britain after the war and addressing the new challenges of the emerging Cold War between the United States and the Soviet Union.

Churchill also played a significant role in the early stages of European integration. He called for a "United States of Europe" to ensure peace and stability on the continent. Although he did not live to see the full realization of this vision, his ideas laid the groundwork for the European Union we know today.

Throughout his post-war years, Churchill continued to be a respected statesman and a powerful voice for freedom and democracy. He remained active in politics until he retired in 1955, but his influence extended far beyond his political career.

Churchill was not only a great leader but also a talented writer. He wrote many books and gave powerful speeches about history. Because of his excellent writing, he won a very special award called the Nobel Prize in Literature in 1953. This prize is given to people who do an outstanding job in writing, and Churchill was one of them!

As Churchill grew older, he spent more time painting and writing, enjoying the quieter moments of life. He passed away in 1965, leaving behind a legacy that continues to inspire people around the world. Winston Churchill is remembered not just as a wartime leader, but as a man who stood firm in the face of adversity, fought for what he believed in, and played a crucial role in shaping the modern world.

Today, we look back at Churchill's life and see a man who was a true lionheart. His courage, determination, and unwavering spirit remind us that even in our darkest hours, there is always hope for a brighter future.

The Legacy of a Leader

Winston Churchill's life was like an exciting adventure filled with battles, challenges, and victories. He left behind a legacy that continues to inspire people today. Churchill was known for his bravery, determination, and ability to inspire others. He showed that a true leader stands strong even when things are tough and never gives up hope.

He wasn't just a great leader; he was also a talented writer and speaker. His words were so powerful that he won the Nobel Prize in Literature in 1953.

Churchill received many honors and awards from all over the world for his contributions to peace and leadership. Today, his speeches and writings are still admired, and his life shows us the power of never giving up.

As we finish the story of Winston Churchill, let's remember that his legacy is not just about the past. It's a source of hope and inspiration for the future. Like Churchill, we can all be brave, stand up for what we believe in, and make a difference in the world.

Visit our author page for more children's books, and remember to follow us for updates on new releases, including illustrated storybooks, fun-fact picture books, coloring books, activity books for kids, and more:

Amazon.com/author/88

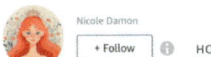
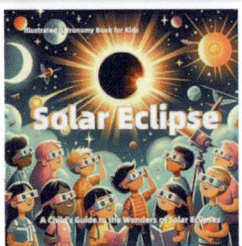

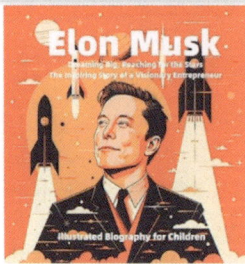
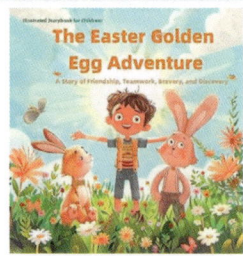

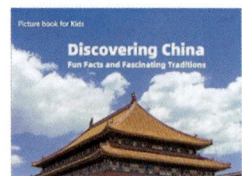

Printed in Great Britain
by Amazon